ART NOUVEAU
ARCHITECTURE AND
FURNITURE

ART NOUVEAU ARCHITECTURE AND FURNITURE

Grange BOOKS

A QUANTUM BOOK

Published by Grange Books
an imprint of Grange Books Plc
The Grange
Kingsnorth Industrial Estate
Hoo, nr. Rochester
Kent ME3 9ND

1-84013-123-3

This book is produced by
Quantum Books Ltd
6 Blundell Street
London N7 9BH

Project Manager: Rebecca Kingsley
Project Editor: Judith Millidge
Designer: Wayne Humphries
Editor: Clare Haworth-Maden

The material in this publication previously appeared in
*Encyclopedia of Decorative Arts, Illustrated History of
Antiques, A Guide to Art Nouveau Style, Introduction to the
Decorative Arts*

QUMANAF
Set in Times
Reproduced in Singapore by Eray Scan Pte Ltd
Printed in Singapore by Star Standard Industries (Pte) Ltd

CONTENTS

AN INTRODUCTION TO ART NOUVEAU

The 19th century had seen enormous changes in society in both Europe and America, with the spread of industrialisation resulting in the creation of great wealth concentrated on the new industrial and commercial cities. The mass production methods of factories not only created a whole new class of workers, but also made a vast range of goods more widely available than ever before. Art Nouveau, which reached its zenith in the early years of the 20th century, began as a reaction against the horrors of mass production, reintroducing skills and craftsmanship which were fast dying out.

Far left: Embroidery by Hermann Orbrist. The love of the undulating line is the purest expression of Art Nouveau.

Below: The Hotel Solvay from 1894-98 in Brussels by Victor Horta.

The essence of Art Nouveau is a line, a sinuous extended curve found in every design of this style. Art Nouveau rejected the order of straight line and right-angle in favour of a more natural movement. Whether these lines were used in realistic descriptions of natural forms, or as abstracted shapes evoking an organic vitality, the emphasis was on decorative pattern and also flatness, a surface on which this concern for the linear, the line of Art Nouveau could be exploited. This curving, flowing line brought with it a feeling of airy lightness, grace and freedom.

The characteristic curving firms of Art Nouveau first appeared in England, yet they were to spread rapidly throughout Europe to a wide range of cities, each with a distinctive interpretation of the style: Paris and Nancy in France, Munich, Berlin and Darmstadt in Germany, Brussels, Barcelona, Glasgow and Vienna all became focal points for the style that was soon universal in Europe, and – with centres in New York and Chicago – equally influential in America.

ORIGINS OF THE NAME

The term itself, Art Nouveau, derives from a Parisian shop of the same name run by a

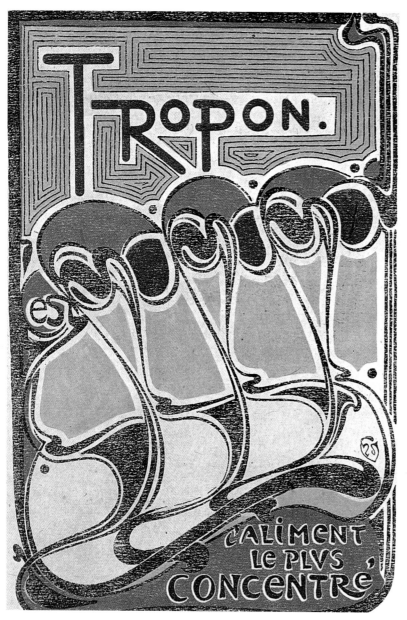

German émigré, Samuel Bing. Bing had been trading for ten years in Japanese art when, in 1895, he re-opened his premises as La Maison de l'Art Nouveau and started to show the work of contemporary designers as well as painters and sculptors. The mixture of gallery, shop and showroom became the Parisian base for the new style, encouraging Bing to commission works for the shop and to promote his artists and craftsmen abroad. Another Italian term for the style, *Stile Liberty,* was attributed to Liberty & Co., the London department store that sold the designs of progressive British craftsmen.

SPREADING THE NEW STYLE

Art Nouveau was not restricted to a few enlightened retailers. The style was also spread by the great international trade fairs of the era. The depth of interest shown by the public in the new fashions in art, and particularly the decorative arts, was also reflected in the huge numbers of new magazines and periodicals devoted to these trends which appeared in the Art Nouveau era.

TRADE FAIRS

The international trade fairs were products of the great age of industrialisation, for they were descended from the 1851 London Great Exhibition, housed in the Crystal Palace, which had been held to demonstrate the possible applications of new technology. These exhibitions soon became an increasingly important feature of international commerce, at which the new styles of decorative art could be displayed. Particularly important events in the develop-

Left: The 'Tropon' poster by the Belgian designer, Henry Van de Velde, from 1898.

ment of Art Nouveau were the international exhibitions of 1899 and 1900 in Paris, and of 1902 in Turin, while that of 1905, held in Liège, marked the end of the style's importance.

ART MAGAZINES

In Germany, it was the influential Munich-based journal *Jugend* (youth) which gave the name '*Jugendstil*' to the German version of Art Nouveau. At the same time, however, the widely read English, and later American periodical, *The Studio* also led to the style being called '*Studiostil*'. Equivalent influential publications were *Pan* from Berlin and *Ver Sacrum* from Vienna. The German language periodicals also included contemporary literature, poetry and criticism, but as in all such journals of the time, the main coverage of the new style came not in specific articles but in the actual design of the publication itself. The title-page, typeface and illustrations were all the work of Art Nouveau graphic artists.

Such periodicals had a wide circulation beyond the limited circle of craftsmen, but there existed too, journals such as the influential *Art et Decoration* from Paris which concentrated more exclusively on the decorative arts, and included many photographs. Thus, through exhibitions, shops, galleries and magazines the Art Nouveau style spread rapidly through Europe and America, both feeding off and stimulating the public's interest.

ORIGINS OF THE STYLE

Because of the wide range of regional styles which resulted in a confusion of different

Right: German advertisement for Bing's gallery and shop, La Maison de L'Art Nouveau, which gave the movement its most popular name.

Above: Part of the French section of the Paris Exposition Universelle of 1900. While technologically advanced, the quality of design had stagnated or even regressed. Bombastic, clumsy, revivalist pieces, such as this furniture, horrified critics such as Ruskin and Morris.

names for the style – '*Art Nouveau*' and '*Modern Style*' in France, '*Modernismo*' in Spain, '*Stile Liberty*' and '*Moderne Stile*' in Italy or even a reference to a place as with '*Belgische Stil*' (Belgium Style) in Germany – there was no clear idea as to common origin, nor shared characteristics, until Art Nouveau was in decline. It is only with hindsight that a more coherent view of the period has been formed.

The origins of Art Nouveau lay mainly in Britain, where the Victorian ornamental de-

signer Christopher Dresser was one of the first to recognise the potency of eccentric curves. In 1862 he wrote: 'A section of the outline of an ellipse is a more beautiful curve than that of an arc since its origin is less apparent, being traced from two centres.'

By common consensus, the first true example of Art Nouveau design was the title page by Arthur Mackmurdo (1851-1942) for his book *Wren's City Churches*, published in 1883. The floral designs of William Morris and the

Arts and Crafts Movement were also influential in formulating the Art Nouveau look.

MORRIS AND THE ARTS AND CRAFTS MOVEMENT

Morris began his career firstly as a painter, as a follower of the Pre-Raphaelites and their dreamy interpretation of the medieval past. However, Morris had a more practical view of that period when it came to his attempt to recreate its idyll of painters, architects and craftsmen working together, often on the same tasks: in 1861 he founded a company to produce the type of objects he wanted to see in every home. This became Morris and Co., and Morris was able to effect a genuine bridging of the divide between artists and craftsmen by employing his Pre-Raphaelite painter-friends to decorate cabinets and bureaux, and to design tapestries, fabrics and chairs.

The actual appearance of these goods was often reminiscent of medieval models, particularly in furniture, but in fabrics, carpets, wallpaper and decoration the Morris style was derived largely from natural sources, inspired by plant, bird and animal forms. The use of hand-crafted, natural materials made these goods too expensive for ordinary people, yet despite this, Morris still hoped that his products would become widespread enough to improve the quality of the lives of as many people as possible. Like the influential writer John Ruskin, Morris hoped to free the working man from the drudgery of factory labour and, through craftsmanship, enable him to gain pleasure from his work.

The example of the Morris Company encouraged other similar enterprises in Britain, usually referred to under the general term 'Arts

Right: The German magazine Jugend, *with cover design by Otto Eckmann.*

and Crafts Movement'. Chief among these was the Century Guild formed in 1884 by Arthur Mackmurdo. Influenced by the flowing, natural forms of Morris, Mackmurdo developed these shapes into elongated, increasingly elegant patterns, and was the first to produce the characteristic vocabulary of sinuous flame-like shapes that were to be the hallmark of Art Nouveau for the next 20 years.

NATURE AND NATURAL FORMS
Nature was to be the ultimate source book of the Art Nouveau artist, particularly the plant world, for many artists had a scientist's depth of knowledge of botany. Flowers, stems and leaves were chosen for their curving silhouettes. Naturally, lilies, irises and orchids were favoured, although any and every form, from palm fronds to seaweed, offered potential for development into an animated pattern.

Insects and birds of colour and grace lent themselves to the same stylising and refining process – dragonflies, peacocks, swallows, or creatures such as snakes or greyhounds. These decorative possibilities could also be developed from the curves of the female body, particularly when combined with long, loose, flowing hair which could be arranged into a fantasy of curls and waves. As the style developed, the quest for more novel forms grew.

HISTORICAL INFLUENCES
Despite the novel qualities of Art Nouveau, some of its stylistic features can be traced to past styles. The Gothic revival served in some ways as an inspiration, for the fervent examination of medieval art of the 19th century

Left: Pan, *the Berlin magazine which covered the same combination of visual arts and literature as* Jugend *did in Munich.*

Above: The title page for Arthur Heygate Mackmurdo's Wren's City Churches.

Left: Cover for Deutsche Kunst und Dekoration, *designed by Margaert Macdonald Mackintosh.*

had emphasised the value of curving, organically-inspired shapes seen in the architecture, sculpture and stained glass of the Middle Ages. As appreciation of the Gothic grew, so too did the awareness that this term encompassed a number of different styles, from the chaste, plain lines of its early period to the flamboyant fantasy of later medieval art. It was this form of the style that was to inspire Art Nouveau. The late Gothic style was plundered not to afford pedantic historical detail, but as

Above: Silver and glass pendant-brooch by René Lalique, c.1900.

Right: 'The Strawberry Thief', a Morris textile design from 1883. Unlike the more abandoned lines of Art Nouveau, the curving natural shapes are here, more symmetrically ordered.

a sourcebook for new ideas.

If flamboyant, late Gothic provided an example of the creative use of the past by the Art Nouveau, then so too did the inspired re-examination of the 18th century rococo style in France. This style had become one of the many open to revivalists of the next century, but rather than resurrect it completely, Art Nouveau observed its forms and characteris-

tics with an independent eye. Rococo had been more broadly associated with the use of capriciously cavorting, light and delicate line as an ornament in all the decorative arts. This was very close to the line of Art Nouveau, and the connection became clear when in France the designers of the regional Nancy school began to incorporate references to rococo in their work.

The common source of natural forms of plant

and wave in both Art Nouveau and rococo made the blend harmonious. The rococo taste for light, high-keyed colour in interiors was also pursued by Art Nouveau, in reaction to the heaviness and solemnity of sombre Victorian interiors. While at its strongest in France, Munich had also been an important outpost of rococo in the 18th century, and it is no coincidence to find that the lightest, wit-

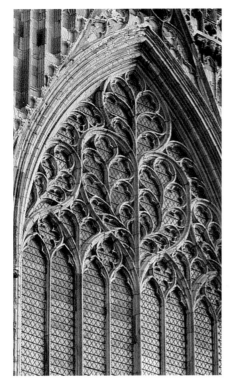

Above: The flamboyant late Gothic style served as an inspiration to Art Nouveau.

Right: The restless line of 18th century Rococo influenced many Art Nouveau designers.

tiest and most fanciful forms of *Jugendstil* were later to be found in that city in the work of Hermann Obrist (1863-1927) or August Endell (1871-1925).

Some stylistic revivals of the late 19th century were partly inspired by the growing nationalism of the time, which was tinged, as ever, by a romantic idea of the past. Some

Above: Detail of a Viking wood carving.

Left: Detail of the doors for the Willow Tea Rooms, designed by C.R Mackintosh.

of the revivals of national artistic consciousness also percolated into Art Nouveau and helped to form its many regional variations. An important influence on the Glasgow school and on its most renowned figure, Charles Rennie Mackintosh, was the revival of interest in early Celtic art.

Celtic jewellery and the ancient gospel books of Durrow, Lindisfarne and Kells revealed precisely their elaborately curving and twisting decoration, the combination of stylisation and the natural inspiration that typified Art Nouveau itself. More particularly, the use of lavish ornament confined within strict limits and contrasted with more open areas had strong parallels with the work of the 19th century Glasgow designers.

With its capricious use of past and peculiar mixture of styles, Art Nouveau could not be anything other than a uniquely novel style.

BELGIUM AND FRANCE

Above: Iron used not only as a decorative element on the balconies, but as a structural framework

Right: The iron and glass vaulting of Brighton Railway Station typifies the use of these materials by engineers before they entered the mainstream of Art Nouveau Architecture.

Overleaf: The vaulted hall from Viollet-le-Duc's Entretiens sur l'Architecture.

Architecture provides the backdrop against which all the varied creations of Art Nouveau can be set. The interdependence between the fine and decorative arts in Art Nouveau is best seen via the works of the major architects of the time, who required fittings in keeping with their domestic architecture while their fellow craftsmen needed the appropriate setting to display their work. From among the fine arts it is architecture that has the strongest technical, craft base, and when the conventional crafts were in decline in the face of industrialisation architects were at the forefront of their revival and, not surprisingly, the leaders of Art Nouveau were also architects: Horta, Guimard, Van de Velde, Behrens, Mackintosh, Gaudi, Gaillard and Grasset.

MODERN MATERIALS FOR A MODERN STYLE

While the architects of the Arts and Crafts movement looked back to a nostalgic pre-industrial era of simple brick and stone homes inspired by the rich traditions of English architecture, the architecture of Art Nouveau began from an opposing premise. Instead of rejecting the industrially produced materials of iron and glass, now more readily available and so dramatically demonstrated in the Crystal Palace erected for the 1851 Great Exhibition in London, the architects of Art Nouveau eagerly embraced the possibilities these modern materials suggested. Consequently, Art Nouveau architecture was to become an important basis for later 20th century developments, and paved the way for the Modern Movement.

FROM ENGINEERING TO ARCHITECTURE

The use of iron to provide strong and comparatively light frames for buildings was first developed in the architecture of the railways and other related industries. It was clear that its strength would inevitably lead to its use in more traditional architecture too, but in England, where iron had been most dramatically used, the development was tentative. The art critic John Ruskin's distaste for industrial materials was a strong influence and when iron was used, its structural role was hidden as much as possible by the more conventional brick and stone.

GOTHIC STYLE

In France however, the architect and theorist Eugène Viollet-le-Duc had no qualms in recommending the open use of iron work in his writings, realising its suitability for the high vaults of his favoured Gothic style and, very significantly, suggesting ways in which it could be shaped to create foliage patterns to embellish its role as a structural element. Excited by the industrial architecture he saw, Viollet-le-Duc was prompted to write in his *Entretiens sur l'architecture* about the further uses of iron and to produce a design for the combination of iron and stained glass. This combination of materials used to create lightness and colour recommended it to the proponents of the new style, while the exploitation of the initial malleability of iron

Right: A detail of the base of the Eiffel Tower, Paris showing some of the ornament which embellishes what is still today, a great feat of engineering.

to create naturalistic ornament was to be of the greatest significance for Art Nouveau architects.

GUSTAVE EIFFEL

The great engineer Gustave Eiffel also carried the influence of English engineering to France. Increasingly involved in the design of pavilions at the numerous international exhibitions, Eiffel allowed more and more of the supporting metal frame to be revealed. It was for the Paris Exhibition of 1889 that his most famous and daring creation, the Eiffel Tower, was produced. When this was allowed to remain after the dismantling of the exhibition, the tower became an important, if controversial monument to the possibilities of the new medium. In the manner of Viollet-le-Duc,

Eiffel had also attempted to embellish his engineering masterpiece with some decorative flourishes in iron.

ART NOUVEAU EMERGES

It was in the fast expanding, and highly developed artistic climate of the Belgian capital of Brussels that an architectural style began to evolve in the works of the highly influential architect Victor Horta (1861-1947). Horta's early work had been with his employer, the academically classical architect Alphonse Balat who had built the imposing Musée Royal des Beaux-Arts.

In 1892 Horta began his Tassel House at 6 Rue Paul-Emile. The Tassel House could not contrast more strongly with the ponderous official architecture. In the interior Horta ex-

posed the iron columns in the hall and stairwell that carried so much of the building's weight and refused to conceal them with brick or plaster. The slender forms of the columns were given a treatment entirely Art Nouveau in character. Rather than mould them into conventional Gothic or classical columns, Horta shaped these supports to resemble the stems of some fantastic vegetation. At capital level Horta attached numerous twisting and turning metal fronds, as if the main column had sprouted growths. The design of the metal was echoed in the linear tendril decoration of the walls and ceilings and repeated again in the mosaic pattern of the floor. These features and the pale colour scheme gave the building an air of freshness, vitality and movement.

Right: The gently curving facade and the large windows, of Victor Horta's classic Art Nouveau Hotel Solvay. The ironwork of the balconies and window mullions provides the only decoration.

Some of the furniture designed by Horta for the Tassel House was, however, less innovative than the building itself. A buffet, for example, with glazed cupboards at each end surmounted by S-scroll pediments and carrying a pair of candelabra with several curling arms, would not have looked out of place in a rococo setting. On the other hand, the profusion of curved stretchers and supports under chairs and tables were pure Art Nouveau.

Having mastered the 'whiplash' line in the Tassel House, Horta began to develop his style through a number of commissions. The Hotel Solvay (1894), originally designed as a private residence, is the most successful of his surviving facades. Essentially, it is a gentle curve between two framing bays supported by exposed iron columns and almost entirely glazed. Horta tried to lighten the effect of his architecture as much as possible with large windows, wide doorways and open stairwells giving an impression of open airy space to his interiors. Now commonplace, it is easy to overlook the immensely refreshing effect that these rooms must have had after the gloom of a Victorian interior.

There is little decoration on the exterior stonework of the Hotel Solvay. Instead, it is the ironwork of the balconies that embellish the building, while their curving effect is continued in the panels of the main door and inside, with the banisters, handles and light fittings all designed by Horta. The latter fall from the ceiling like inverted creepers whose flowers are the shades for the electric light

Above: Horta's airy interiors were achieved by the use of glass ceilings and splendid iron columns.

bulbs. Horta's attention to detail was such that all the fittings in the house, right down to the furniture and the locks for the doors, continued the organic, curvilinear theme.

In 1898-1900 Horta designed his own studio and house, the Atelier and Maison Horta-now the Musée Horta in Brussels. At the same time, his structural and exterior design became increasingly adventurous, and his most ambitious work of this period is the now demolished Maison du Peuple of 1897. A vast social centre, the large auditorium of this building was supported on a metal frame that was entirely exposed- a daring and modern device that was balanced by the smooth curves of the iron ribs, beams and balconies. Built almost entirely of metal and glass, the facade was a sweeping concave of interlaced ironwork and massed elliptical windows.

Horta's style moderated progressively through the 1890s, and by 1905 he had virtually abandoned the Art Nouveau style. His furniture however, is characterised by its abstract forms derived from nature and by its rather thin, spindly structural members. Horta also created the idea of built-in furniture, which became such a typical feature of the Art Nouveau interior that the French writer Edmond Goncourt invented for it the sobriquet 'Yachting Style'; a banquette, for example, would run along one wall, turn a corner and finish as a display case.

VAN DER VELDE

Another Belgian, Henri Van de Velde (1863-1957), first experimented with the Art Nouveau style through typography and book decoration. He progressed to interior decoration with the Hotel Otlet in 1894, and a year later built his own house at Bloemenwerf near Uccle, for which he designed all the furniture himself.

In marked contrast to Horta's flamboyant townhouse, it incorporated Art Nouveau lines into a rural idiom, with striped gables and shuttered windows. The furniture incorporated features derived from Arts and Crafts practices, and Horta's curvilinear style. Some pieces were made of oak, and some were simply constructed rush-seated side chairs. But more elaborate pieces were decorated with carved ornament in a forceful Art Nouveau idiom.

Van de Velde went on to design interiors for Bing's Paris shop, office furniture for the German art critic Julius Meier-Graefe, as well as pieces for the German firm of Loffler, before moving to Germany where he set up the Weimar School of Arts and Crafts which subsequently became the Bauhaus.

THE FRENCH MASTERS

In France, the official training college for architects, designers and fine-art students, the Ecole des Beaux-Arts, represented the old historicising tendency at its coldest and most academic. The compulsion to imitate is encapsulated in Charles Garnier's Paris Opera House, built between 1861 and 1876, which is regarded by its more vehement critics as a worthless exercise in plagiarism. The theories of Viollet-le-Duc regarding the 'honest' use of iron – leaving it exposed rather than hiding it with terracotta and other fake masonry – were to prove particularly influential to French architects of Art Nouveau. Of these, the greatest exponent was Hector Guimard (1867-1942). While Horta limited his plant-like decoration mostly to interiors, and even treated it with a certain coolness, Guimard allowed fantasy to dominate his work. At times

Right: A cabinet by Horta for his own house in Brussels.

he seemed to be deliberately challenging the accepted limitations of his medium, whether it was iron, wood or stone.

Based on the ideas of Viollet-le-Duc, but without using any form of overtly Gothic style, Guimard produced quaint, rustic chalets such as the Castel Henriette, with pitched roofs and a restless sense of movement in the forms of gables, doors and windows. The informality of his out-of-town architecture is also well demonstrated in the Villa Henri Sauvage built for the designer Louis Majorelle, outside Nancy. The house, with its high gables, assertive asymmetry and details of chimney pots and balconies, approaches a fairytale whimsy. Only hinted at here, the verticality of Gothic was often very near the surface of French Art Nouveau architecture, as in the work of Charles Plumet who liked to use steeply-roofed dormer windows and pointed arches, or in the

Above: Bloemenwerf, Van de Velde's residence in Uccle, Brussels, 1895-96.

Right: Interior of the Paris shop, La Maison Moderne, designed by Van de Velde for Julius Meier-Graefe in 1898.

town house that jewellery designer René Lalique created for himself by adapting the vocabulary of French chateaux architecture.

If Guimard's country villas had a sort of rural quaintness, then his Parisian work is more forceful. In building his own house on the Avenue Mozart, he carved the stonework into the most dramatic forms, no longer simply just natural in origin, suggesting trees and plants, but exaggerated into a more artificial fantasy and elegance.

Guimard's concern for detail was equal to that of Horta. In this house as well as in his major apartment block, the Castel Beranger finished in 1898, his designs in metalwork and stained glass are particularly notable. In these he created purely abstract forms, emphasised by the terracotta panels decorating the entrance of the building, which ooze and flow across the walls as if they were still molten.

The furniture that Guimard designed for the Castel Beranger reflects his adherence to the principles of rational design taught by Viollet-le-Duc. Its construction, although visually flamboyant, is always justifiable in terms of strength and utility. The wave-like linear decoration carved in low relief is abstract, but clearly inspired by natural forms.

'STYLE MÉTRO'
Unlike Horta, Guimard worked in cast as well as wrought-iron, and it was the former that provided the basic material for the numerous Métro entrances and ticket offices he designed from 1900. Inspired works of fantasy, the entrances for the Paris Métro gave Guimard his most public prominence and even resulted in a local variation of Art Nouveau, the 'Style Métro'.

Right: A pearwood cabinet designed by architect, Hector Guimard, c.1900.

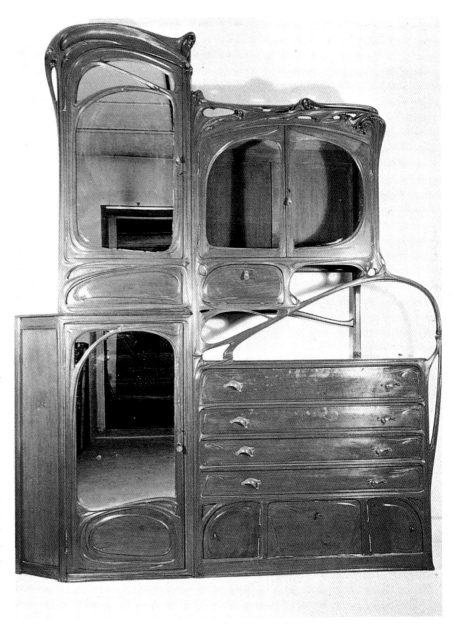

Above: The entrance to Guimard's Castel Beranger, where stone is carved to create the impression of a malleable material.

Left: An occasional table by Hector Guimard showing the same sinuous shapes as his entrances for the Paris Metro.

While the overhead structures of the Métro in the suburbs had been given a thoroughly conventional treatment – incidentally earning a decoration for their architect – Guimard was commissioned to produce shelters and archways for the entrances to the underground sections. These were so startlingly Art Nouveau that they provoked considerable controversy.

In keeping with the modernity of the new underground railway, Guimard restricted himself to the use of iron, enamelled steel and glass. The iron elements were produced in a large number of standard parts, making their assembly into a huge variety of arches and pavilions, a tribute to Guimard's inventiveness and versatility. The treatment of the ironwork was typically curvilinear, with barely a straight line to be seen in the whole design. Lamps sprouted from metal branches and the word 'Métropolitain' itself was carefully composed into harmonious Art Nouveau forms. Some of these amazing ironwork shapes, although organic in feel, had an angular tension strangely reminiscent of bones, and lacked the fluid grace of much of Guimard's interior designs, and of French Art Nouveau as a whole.

MÉTRO

While best known for the Métro entrances, Guimard's masterpiece was in fact the Humbert de Romans concert hall, built in 1898 and destroyed just seven years later as Art Nouveau quickly went out of fashion. Its crowning glory was a domed roof composed of steel ribs supporting a cupola pierced with windows of yellow stained glass.

ARCHITECTS: DESIGNERS AND CRAFTSMEN

Art Nouveau furniture bears all the variety of the regional styles of the movement. True to the spirit of Art Nouveau, few craftsmen specialised exclusively in furniture, and most had been trained in other arts or crafts. Most Art Nouveau furniture makers had been, or remained, architects, concerned to extend their control over the interiors of their buildings. The same tensions between ornament and structure, form and function were as evident in furniture-making as in architecture.

Right: Paris Metro, Bois de Boulogne, by Hector Guimard, 1900.

Right: Side chair in walnut by Eugene Gaillard, c.1900. The forms are inspired by nature, but are not in direct imitation of it.

Far right: Console table by Georges de Feure. The forms are pure Art Nouveau but the gilding betrays an 18th inspiration.

LES SIX

In 1897 a group of artists calling themselves *Les Six* held an exhibition in Paris which included furniture designed by the architect Charles Plumet and the brothers Pierre and Tony Selmersheim. Their work was Art Nouveau in style, often with a strong flavour of the rococo in its sinuous lines and gilt metal fittings which often alluded to natural forms. Another member of Les Six, the sculptor Alexandre Charpentier, (1856-1909) was a furniture designer who achieved his main effects by the treatment of wood, with gilt-bronze reliefs and colour. The wood was carved to give it a molten, sometimes almost liquid, appearance; the relief panels, handles and lock-plates represented female nudes; and the wood itself, – usually hornbeam – was waxed to give it a yellow tint, somewhere between gold and honey.

Jean Dampt, another sculptor who belonged to the group, was a disciple of John Ruskin and an admirer of the English Arts and Crafts Movement. His furniture is Art Nouveau with Neo-Gothic touches.

SAMUEL BING'S GALERIE DE L'ART NOUVEAU

In Paris, Samuel Bing's Galerie de l'Art Nouveau was the principle showcase for Art Nouveau furniture, as for other crafts. Reflecting the nationalism fashionable at the time in France, Bing encouraged the crafts-

men who worked for him to study the great French tradition of 'grace, elegance, purity and sound logic', and principally the refined poise of 18th century work. Bing showed a great range of work but he favoured a nucleus of three furniture makers: Eugène Gaillard, Georges de Feure and Edward Colonna.

Gaillard represents the functional side of Art Nouveau furniture; he studied the problem of function in design and produced pieces of an increasingly light, almost classic, simplicity. His chairs were concerned with comfort, had moulded backs, sometimes padding at the shoulders, and leather or fabric-covered coil-sprung upholstered seats.

THE PARIS WORLD'S FAIR

George de Feure, a painter and poet, was something of a dandy. he was a keeper of grey-

hounds, which he admired for their fine Art Nouveau lines. He brought more colour and decoration to his furniture, with gilding and coloured lacquer, as well as the kind of carved detail rare in Gaillard's work.

The third, Edward Eugène Colonna, had emigrated from Cologne to America where he worked under Tiffany, before returning to Europe to continue his career in Paris. Colonna's furniture, like de Feure's, was part of a larger output including porcelain and fabrics, and had a delicate, attenuated elegance also close to de Feure's style. When Bing was honoured with his own pavilion devoted to Art Nouveau at the 1900 Paris World's Fair, these three designers were given the task of decorating and furnishing it.

THE NANCY SCHOOL

Aside from Guimard and his contemporaries working in Paris, France had a second school of Art Nouveau architects working at Nancy in Lorraine in eastern France, at a colony led by the designer Emile Gallé (1846-1904). Its outstanding achievement in architecture was the Villa Majorelle of 1900, which was designed chiefly by Henri Sauvage.

Nancy was historically the home of the glass-making industry and Gallé, heir to a small ceramic and glassware business became the leader of the Art Nouveau revival of the city's main industry. In the 1870s Gallé had travelled to England and had been caught up in the growing enthusiasm for the decorative arts. He also studied the oriental collection at the Victoria and Albert Museum in London and, with his new found knowledge of Chinese and Japanese techniques, he returned to Nancy.

Gallé also possessed a specialist's understanding of botany and entomology, his other amateur passions. Thus he was equipped with

a very detailed first-hand knowledge of leaf, flower and insect forms, which, when combined with the decorative, abstract tendency of the Japanese, combined to form the Art Nouveau blend. A third ingredient, rococo, was already evident in Nancy, which had many fine houses and decorations in that style.

Above: A rare use of fantastic grotesques by Emile Gallé Characteristically, the whole table leg is given over to their form.

GALLÉ AND FURNITURE DESIGN

In 1884, after some years designing in glass and ceramics, Gallé started designing and producing furniture. At first his designs were somewhat ponderous but were invariably enlivened with vivid natural details. Success came at the 1889 Paris International Exhibition, where Gallé was acknowledged as an innovator, who had created a new style in reaction to the unimaginative revivalism of most contemporary French furniture.

Gallé's work became increasingly lighter and more ornate. Natural forms were not restricted to details; whole arms, legs and backs were carved in plant or insect forms, curving and twisting to animate the whole and seeming to defy the nature of the wood itself. Although stylised, those graceful shapes were always clearly identifiable plants of species

Left: An armchair, c.1900 by the Nancy cabinet maker, Louis Majorelle.

Below: A carved fruit wood and marquetry tray c.1900 by Emile Gallé.

known to Gallé. His favourites were local plants including cow-parsley, water lilies, orchids and irises, though he also used exotics, such as bamboo.

Gallé preferred soft woods, of which he had a very thorough knowledge, to facilitate the creation of is effects, which included his remarkable revival of the art of marquetry. Most of the surfaces of Gallé's furniture become fields for the most intricate inlays featuring plants, insects or landscapes in what could become an overloading of effects. So fine was the craftsmanship though, that Gallé's own willowy signature could be reproduced on his pieces.

MARQUETRY

Gallé's mastery of marquetry opened the way to the expression of poetry and literary themes in his furniture. He liked to include suitable quotations and, as a mark of the fusion of the arts and crafts in Art Nouveau, he gave some pieces names in the manner of paintings or music. A console he created became *Les Parfums d'Autrefois* (Perfumes of the Past) and his last masterpiece, a bed he designed while dying of leukaemia, *Aube et Crepescule* (Dawn and Dusk). This latter piece is evidence of Gallé's increasing restraint in his late style, simplifying forms and eradicating much of the over-intricacy of his earlier work, as well as being a tour-de-force of marquetry. The dark shadows of dusk are enveloped in the drooping wings of the fantastic insect on the headboard, while at the foot of the bed, the rising wings of another huge insect are depicted in lighter woods and mother-of-pearl.

Second to Gallé at the Nancy School was Louis Majorelle (1859-1929). Majorelle began designing in an 18th-century style until Gallé persuaded him to inject more vitality and naturalism into his work. His pieces are, nevertheless, rather more solid than Gallé's, partly because he favoured the use of harder, more exotic woods. The more sculptural elements in Majorelle's pieces were in the ornamentation, which, still partly inspired by the baroque and rococo, he added in gilt, copper or bronze. Majorelle equalled Gallé in his use of marquetry, but generally his style differs in its smoother lines. Majorelle was consequently able to make a successful transition to the simpler style of the 1920s.

CABINET MAKERS

Other cabinet makers in Nancy worked for either Gallé or Majorelle, and occasionally both. Victor Prouve (1858-1943) specialised in marquetry work for both masters as well as designing his own pieces. Eugène Vallin (1856-1925) worked for Gallé and produced pieces of far greater weight than those of his master. Vallin's work eschews intricate natural detail and instead concentrates on broad, swaying, linear rhythms anticipating the end of his career when he took up architecture and used cast concrete for his effects. Jacques Gruber produced designs for Majorelle and was also Professor of Decorative Arts at the Ecole des Beaux-Arts in Nancy. His furniture shares the same flowing forms as that of Vallin, and is removed from Gallé's rococo touches.

Through a range of Art Nouveau furniture it is possible to see designs stripped down to the most elegant bare curves, as well as those which are adorned with carving, brass, gilt or ivory. A similar contrast exists between designs that are obviously designed for comfort and utility, and those that come close to sacrificing both these concerns for the sake of effect. What gives coherence to this variety are the irrepressible curves and sense of idiosyncratic inventiveness. Occasionally these had

Above: Office suite by Eugene Vallin in exaggerated Art Nouveau style.

to be curbed especially when designs were intended for mass production. The attention to detail and the manipulation of the materials generally meant that Art Nouveau furniture was unsuited to any mode of production other than that of the individual craftsman. As in the Arts and Crafts Movement in England, the Art Nouveau designer was forced to accept the fact that his work was primarily an expensive luxury for an élite. Factory-produced Art Nouveau furniture inevitably lost much of its natural vitality and was a coarsened version of the hand-worked equivalent. Art Nouveau architects might have been eager to embrace the new materials of iron and steel, but when they turned to designing furniture their style was fundamentally unsuited to modern production techniques.

Below: Furniture designed as part of a unified environment by the Parisian Georges Hoentschel.

BRITAIN, AUSTRIA AND GERMANY

U nlike the French and the Belgians, the architects and designers of Britain, Austria and Germany used the languid curves of Art Nouveau with great austerity, and in harmonious counterpoint to grid-like patterns of horizontal and vertical lines.

Overleaf: Interior of Hill House, Dunbartonshire, Scotland designed by C.R Mackintosh, 1904.

Below: Oak side chairs by E.W Pugin, c.1870 conform to the principles of simplicity and clear construction advocated by his father, the architect and critic A.W. N. Pugin.

THE INFLUENCE OF THE ARTS AND CRAFTS MOVEMENT

From the 1860s onwards Britain rose to a prominent position in European decorative arts. The founding of Morris, Marshall, Faulkner & Co. in 1861 had been the beginning of a new movement in reaction to the allegorical flourishes of design in the 1851 Great Exhibition. The Arts and Crafts Movement, absorbing the tenets of the Gothic Revival, was committed to honest and simple design for domestic use. Inspired by the teachings of John Ruskin and Pre-Raphaelite artists, the majority of the designers were professional architects. It was also an intellectual movement, which successfully captured the imagination of the time.

Arts and Crafts furniture laid stress on the honest presentation of materials, structure and production, taking as its highest principle

Ruskin and William Morris's belief that only the highest good could come from man transforming his own environment with his own hands. The machine was despised, as was any decorative idiom which slavishly copied past styles. Handicrafts flourished, especially in the fields of embroidery, metalwork, stained glass and art pottery.

All over the country handicraft guilds were founded to involve both the working man and the hitherto unemployable young lady in the practical creation of their own environment. The most influential of these guilds were the Century Guild founded in 1882by Arthur

Mackmurdo, the Art-Workers' Guild founded in 1884, Charles Robert Ashbee's Guild of Handicraft formed in 1888, the same year as the Arts and Crafts Exhibition Society, and, in 1900 the Birmingham Guild of Handicraft.

SPREADING THE STYLE

The original impetus of the Arts and Crafts ideals gave rise to considerable activity which was chronicled in the pages of *The Studio*. The magazine was frankly propagandist for the movement, and through its pages the inspiration of British design was made known in Europe and America. In 1898 the Grand-

Above: A cabinet decorated with scenes from the life of St George, painted by William Morris. The medievalism of the piece is typical of the furniture produced by Morris & Co during the 1860s.

Right: The Honeysuckle Room at Wightwick Manor. Carpets, wallpaper, tiles and furniture by Morris & Co.

Duke of Hesse commissioned designs from Charles Ashbee and M.H Baillie Scott for furniture, made by the Guild of Handicraft, for the artist's colony set up at Darmstadt. Britain's lead was beginning to take effect abroad.

Yet despite leading the way in the decorative arts, Britain, however, was to strongly oppose any new influences such as Art Nouveau, and remained firm in her adherence to the simple functional lines and country morals of the Arts and Crafts Movement. Innovative, artists such as the Glasgow Four, who were acclaimed abroad, were to be virtually ignored by both critics and public alike at home.

CHARLES RENNIE MACKINTOSH AND THE GLASGOW FOUR

The Glasgow Four were Charles Rennie Mackintosh, his wife Margaret, Herbert MacNair and Frances Macdonald (Margaret's sister, who married MacNair), all of whom studied at the Glasgow School of Art in the early 1890s.

Mackintosh (1868-1928), an architect, had produced his first furniture designs in the early 1890s and this early work already shows an avoidance of reference to period design and a sparseness in the absence of applied decoration. Mackintosh's designs were dictated by the problems of the arrangement of interior space and he laid stress on vertical elements, his high-backed chairs giving a variety of height within a room, despite the acknowledged criticism of their impracticality.

In 1896 the Four were invited to send fur-

niture, craftwork and posters to the Arts and Crafts Exhibition Society show where their work, especially the posters, met with a puzzled and shocked reaction. The editor of *The Studio,* however, made a visit to Glasgow and in 1897 published two appreciative articles on their work. This was quickly picked up in Europe and the following year the Darmstadt magazine *Dekorative Kunst* contained an article on the Glasgow School.

MACKINTOSH AND VIENNA

Earlier in 1895, work from Glasgow Art School had been sent to the Liège Exhibition where it was received enthusiastically, although Mackintosh himself never favoured the Belgian and French excesses of Art Nouveau. It was in Vienna that he found like minds.

In 1900 he visited the 8th Vienna Secessionist Exhibition, which was devoted to the work of foreign designers, including Mackintosh and his wife, Charles Ashbee and Henry Van de Velde. There he met Josef Hoffmann with whom he was to remain in contact for many years, warmly supporting the decision to found the *Wiener Werkstätte.* Mackintosh received two commissions in Vienna, including the design of a music room for the banker Fritz Waerndorfer, who was to finance the Werkstätte, where a dining room was commissioned from Hoffmann. Mackintosh also exhibited successfully at the Turin Exhibition of 1902. It must have been a sore disappointment to Mackintosh to find his work received so sympathetically abroad while being almost ignored in Britain. Despite being a very influential figure in late European Art Nouveau, Mackintosh's architectural career is largely confined to the Glasgow School of Art, the series of tea rooms designed for Miss Cranston and a handful of private

Above: Scottish architect and designer, Charles Rennie Mackintosh (1868-1928).

strate his remarkable creation of a distinctive style totally removed from the influences of the preceding century.

MACKINTOSH'S ARCHITECTURE

Mackintosh's first important commission came in 1896, when he won a competition to design a new School of Art for the city of Glasgow. At first sight the building which he constructed over 12 years bears little resemblance to Art Nouveau works elsewhere.

The asymmetry and the hint of the turrets evident in the front entrance refer to Mackintosh's early enthusiasm for the Gothic revival. In the starkly-mullioned great windows of the north-facing studios and the apparent simplicity of the whole, there is evidence of the uniquely British Arts and Crafts architects with their Tudor references.

IRONWORK

Yet Mackintosh is a figure of European significance in Art Nouveau, and his importance extends beyond the local. The curving stonework in the centre of the main facade, and the stylised elongation of the windows of the west front display the refinement of Art Nouveau, and the connection becomes stronger in the details of the building. The carving over the entrance has the curving, Celtic lines of Art Nouveau graphics and metalwork of the Glasgow school, and the ironwork indulges in more abstract curves. This is used to contrast with the harder lines of the stone background in a way reminiscent of Horta's Hotel Solvay. The ironwork, resembling buttresses against the main studio window, is rounded off in intricate, loosely-bound knots of metalwork, almost like enlarged pieces of jewellery. The strange decorations on the railings at street level, and the bundles of arrow shapes

houses for Scottish patrons, notably Hill House, Helensburgh (1902) built for the publisher Walter Blackie. These projects, where he designed almost every element, from cutlery for the tea rooms to rugs for Hill House, demon-

supporting patterned dishes, derive from Japanese heraldry, which emphasise the wide internationalism of Mackintosh's references and his affinity with the orientally-inspired refinements of Art Nouveau.

The simplicity and elegance of Japan are again recalled in the interior of the school's library, completely designed by Mackintosh. He was reluctant to experiment with structural ironwork, so wood is used throughout to support the galleries. Mackintosh's fascination with beams and joints was a typically eclectic Art Nouveau fusion of his Japanese and Gothic interests, and is seen again in the open rafters elsewhere in the building. The use of dark stained wood also gives the library an oriental sobriety. By opening out a continuous airy central space, Mackintosh created slender, vertical beams, which are echoed in the delicate light fittings. It was a variation on one of the great themes of Art Nouveau architecture: the open, light and spacious interior, in this case lit by the long, triple bay windows of the west facade.

MACKINTOSH'S FURNITURE

In furniture, as in architecture, it was Mackintosh's work that dominated British Art Nouveau. Mackintosh's furniture is intended to be seen as part of a whole interior design with secondary work often produced by other artists and designers. Mackintosh's designs show a virtuosity which is breath-taking, if sometimes self-indulgent. It is easy to understand why his furniture was not well received in England where it was regarded with suspicion for being too stylised or 'aesthetic'.

Right: A cover for Deutsche Kunst und Dekoration, *designed by Margaret Macdonald Mackintosh.*

Right: Wall panels and mirrors with stylised plant motifs for Miss Cranston's Willow Tea Rooms in Glasgow, designed by C.R. Mackintosh in 1904. For this project, Mackintosh designed almost every element, from the cutlery to the furniture.

Simplicity was sacrificed to sophistication, tradition was flouted and scant respect was shown for materials. As in his architecture, he concentrated upon the extremely elegant, exaggerated verticals, particularly in the backs of his chairs which could be exceptionally tall and slender. These were cut into ovals, grids or ladderbacks that descended down to the floor. Curves might occur, but with Mackintosh they were primarily used to underline the rigidity of the verticals.

Furniture was made from various woods, including oak, cypress, pine and mahogany, which were rarely left untreated. Mackintosh felt uncomfortable with the natural grain of the wood and attempted to minimise it by deep, dark staining and eventually by lacquering or ebonising it into matt black. He explored a converse neutrality by painting other pieces white to act as a suitable background for lilac and silver harmonies. On lighter furniture, Mackintosh stencilled stylised designs.

While he received great recognition in Germany and Austria (especially among the architects of the Secession) Mackintosh's greatest achievement may have been to point a path forward from the decorative excesses of Art Nouveau, which found itself fading in popularity after the first five years of the 20th century and was laid to rest by the horrors of World War I.

GERMANY AND JUGENDSTIL

Jugenstil (Youth Style) was the German term for Art Nouveau. In Munich during the 1890s, a number of architects, painters and sculptors

Far left: A white-painted table by C.R. Mackintosh. Mackintosh felt uncomfortable with natural grain in wood and attempted to minimise it by staining, lacquering, ebonising and painting the surfaces of his furniture.

Left: A black chair by C.R. Mackintosh. Mackintosh used extremely elegant, exaggerated verticals, particularly in the backs of his chairs which could be exceptionally tall and slender. They were often cut into ovals, ladder-backs that descended to the floor, or, as in this example, into grids.

including Hermann Obrist (1863-1927), August Endell (1871-1921), Richard Riemerschmid (1868-1957), Bernhard Pankok (1872-1943) and Bruno Paul (1874-1954) turned their attention to the applied arts. In 1897, these five, among others founded the *Vereinigte Wekstatten fur Kunst im Handwerk* (United Workshops for Art in the Handicrafts). Obrist and Endell designed furniture in flowing natural forms that were determined by a theory of interaction between physical appearances and psychological reactions. Obrist's furniture was made of oak, and Endell's of elm, while Pankok's designs, which were also based on natural forms, were made of oak, pearwood, walnut and spruce.

NEO-GOTHIC STYLE
Richard Riemerschmid's earliest experiments in furniture were some pieces he designed for his own apartment in 1895. They were in the Neo-Gothic style, made of stained and painted pine and decorated with elaborate wrought-

Right: The Atelier Elvira, 1897-1898, Munich (now destroyed) by August Endell.

Bottom: Table and chair with stencilled back, c.1901 by C.R. Mackintosh.

iron hinges and foliate ornament carved in low relief. However, Riemerschmid's style was to change, as a result of seeing an exhibition at Dresden in 1897of Van de Velde's furniture. His abstract Art Nouveau style made a great impact on all the Munich artists, including Bruno Paul, whose work was characterised by elegant curved lines and was free of any ornamentation. The following year Riemerschmid designed an oak side-chair, its back-rest carried on supports which descend in a sweeping curve to the feet of the front legs.

THE DRESDEN WORKSHOPS

One of the intentions underlying the work of the Munich artists was to create furniture cheap enough for a far larger public than could afford the hand-built furniture produced by the leading avant-garde designers of Paris, Nancy and Brussels. When selecting the forms their furniture would take, the Germans took into account the new wood-working machines being developed at the time. The leader of this tendency was Karl Schmidt, Riemerschmid's brother-in-law, who had trained as a cabinet maker and in 1898 opened the *Dresdner Werkstätten* (Dresden Workshops). At an exhibition of industrial art held in Dresden in 1899-1900, Schmidt showed an apartment of two living rooms, a bedroom and a kitchen, inexpensively furnished with simple modern furniture. Five years later, the *Dresdner Werkstätten* produced a range of machine-made furniture designed by Riemerschmid.

THE GERMAN WORKSHOPS

In 1902 Adelbert Niemeyer, an artist, and Karl Bertsch, an upholsterer, founded a workshop

Left: An oak sideboard by August Endell, c.1900. Endell believed that the shape of an object could induce feelings of serenity.

Below: Dining chair designed by Richard Reimerschmid, c.1900.

in Munich for the manufacture of furniture and other items of interior decoration. In 1907 the workshop merged with the *Dresdner Werkstätten* and the two became known as the *Deutscher Werkstätten* (German Workshop). This should not be confused with the *Deutscher Werkbund* which was an association of designers, craftsmen, manufacturers and retailers promoted by the German government and founded in the same year. Niemeyer continued to design furniture for the *Deutsche Werkstätten* until his death. Other designers who occasionally worked for the Dresden concern include Baillie Scott and the Austrians Josef Hoffmann (1870-1956) and Kolomon Moser (1868-1918).

THE DARMSTADT DESIGNERS
Having been frequently illustrated in *The Studio* magazine, Baillie Scott's work was well known on the continent. These illustrations had caught the eye of the Grand Duke Ernst Ludwig

of Hesse-Darmstadt, who in 1897 had had a drawing room and a dining room in his palace at Darmstadt furnished by Baillie Scott and Charles Ashbee. The Grand Duke encouraged the establishment of an artist's colony in Darmstadt and donated some land for it. Seven artists were invited to join the colony and by 1900 their homes were being built. For his house, Peter Behrens (1868-1940), an architect who had been working in Munich during the 1890s, designed furniture which was close in style to the work of Van de Velde. Josef Maria Olbrich (1867-1908), although from Vienna, was another Darmstadt colonist who created furniture for his own and other artist's houses in a style which was a successful blend of organic shapes and geometrical ornament.

AUSTRIA AND THE SECESSIONISTS
In Austria the Art Nouveau style was called *Secessionstil*, after the Vienna Secession which was formed in 1897 both as a reaction

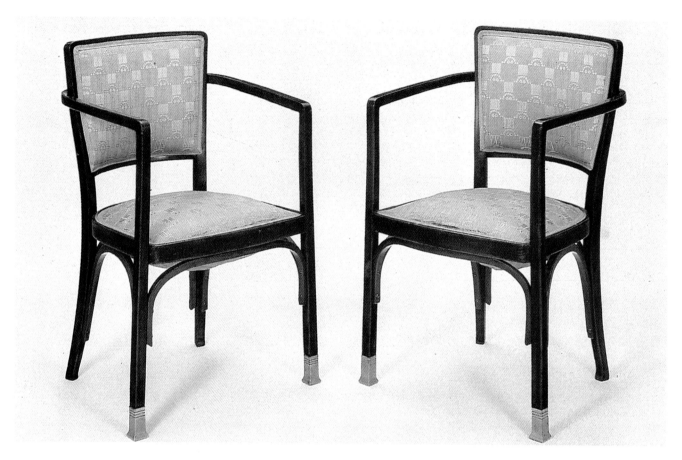

Above: Chairs by Kolomon Moser of the Viennese Secession movement, showing the great restraint of the style, partly inspired by Charles Rennie Mackintosh.

against the tired revivalism of academic artists and as a celebration of modernity. It was therefore almost inevitable that the work of its members should directly reflect the influence of the Art Nouveau style which by then was fully developed in Western Europe. Beginning as something of a local variant on Art Nouveau, this late flowering of the style was to prove a turning point between Art Nouveau opulence and 20th century austerity. Even in their earlier works, the Austrian

architects preferred a framework of straighter lines to set off the opulent curves of Art Nouveau. They were particularly appreciative of these qualities in Mackintosh's style, which helped to form their own, and of the English Arts and Crafts architects, who by this stage were opposing the sensuality of Art Nouveau.

OLBRICH AND THE SECESSIONHAUS
Just as the Arts and Crafts practitioners had lauded the merits of simplicity and honesty

in architecture and design, so too did the group of Austrian architects, painters and sculptors who seceded from the official artists' organisation and held their own exhibitions in the Secessionhaus designed by Josef Maria Olbrich in 1897-99. As a founder member of the breakaway group, Olbrich felt it necessary to make a strong architectural statement. The main structure of the building – reputedly inspired by a rough sketch by the painter Gustav Klimt – is substantial, and complete with concrete facing, but the detailing with animal and vegetable life is an all-important aspect of the building, particularly on the tracery of the iron dome. Like the spires of Cologne's medieval cathedral, the perforated structure lightens the 'weight' of the building. Much of the Secession's work in all art forms, achieved this type of effect through well-controlled contrast, rather than by an unbridled release of free flowing forms.

OTTO WAGNER'S ARCHITECTURE

One of the older Secessionists, Otto Wagner (1841-1918) was an influential writer and theorist. His architectural career had not brought him a great deal of public success, but the Secession supported his pupils Olbrich and Josef Hoffmann. In 1899 Wagner himself became a full member of the Secession, largely severing his connections with much of his own generation and the Vienna Akademie's school of architecture.

MAJOLIKAHAUS

The year before, Wagner had publicly shown his allegiance to the Secession style by his treatment of the façade of an apartment block he had designed, aptly dubbed the 'Majolikahaus'. In essence, this consisted of

Above: A poster advertising one of the annual exhibitions held by the craftsmen of the Vienna Secession.

Left: The Exhibition hall of 1898 designed by Josef Olbrich for the Secession in Vienna.

a completely regular grid of windows, devoid of any architectural or sculptural decoration. However, to counteract the austerity Wagner decorated the whole facade with brightly-coloured majolica, floral patterned tiles that seem to grow up from the second floor, and gradually enveloped the whole building in the light, sinuous lines of Austrian Art Nouveau.

STADTBAHN

Before the establishment of the Secession group, Wagner, with Olbrich as his assistant, was appointed architect to the new Viennese underground and suburban railway, the Stadtbahn. The design of the Stadtbahn stations immediately invite comparison with Guimard's work for the Paris Métro. Wagner's stations lack the free-flowing fantasy of Guimard, yet they have a rather rococo grace and lightness, with abundant floral detailing, which is the closest point in Austrian architecture to the French style of Art Nouveau.

The speed with which Art Nouveau was acknowledged was equalled only by the speed with which it came under criticism. Wagner's Post Office Savings Bank, built between 1904 and 1906 in the centre of Vienna, reveals a completely new aesthetic, based soundly on 'truth to materials'. With austere ornamentation, its structural components such as rivets and nuts provide a wealth of decoration. Here Wagner created a building using up-to-date methods of construction and materials such as steel, aluminium, glass and concrete to create a large, airy main hall. To the contemporary eye, the interior of the building must have appeared somewhat spartan, but in the attention to every

Left: The magnificent Karlsplatz Station of the Vienna Stadtbahn (subway train) designed by Otto Wagner.

Left: Exterior view of the Palais Stoclet, Brussels, designed by Josef Hoffmann and begun in 1905.

detail of furniture and fitting, the light, glass roof and particularly the elegant tapering piers supporting the gently curved vault, all suggest the remaining echoes of Art Nouveau.

THE WIENER WERKSTÄTTE

Wagner's former pupil, Josef Hoffmann, appreciated craftsmanship and believed that ornament had an important role in architecture. Together with Kolomon Moser (1868-1918), Hoffmann established the *Wiener Werkstätte* (Vienna Workshop), a workshop dedicated to the production of functional but beautiful objects.

Hoffmann's Purkersdorf convalescent home (1903) reveals structural sincerity; his designs for the Palais Stoclet in Brussels (1905-11) however, allowed him to put his theories fully into practice. Stoclet, a wealthy financier, commissioned Hoffmann to build a palatial home

that should also serve as a suitable setting for his art collection and for entertaining. What Hoffmann designed was a house of great distinction, combining elements of formality (strong horizontals and verticals) with great informality (an irregular floor plan and a facade that did nothing to hide the irregularity of the room arrangement within). The very asymmetry of the design coupled with the unusual shapes and positions of the windows points strongly to Mackintosh's work.

HOFFMANN'S FURNITURE

Many of Hoffmann's furniture designs also show the influence of Mackintosh, but he maintained a high level of personal inventiveness. Characteristic of Hoffmann's furniture are lattice-like chair backs and table aprons, and small spheres of wood for decoration at points of

structural significance. Hoffmann's style gradually became more retrospective, using some Neo-classical and Biedermeier (an informal 19th century style) forms.

The same influence is evident in the furniture created by two other *Wiener Werkstätten* designers, Otto Prutscher and Josef Urban (1872-1933). While some of the pieces designed by Moser were richly decorated with marquetry or inlaid metals, others, like Mackintosh's in Glasgow, were simply painted white.

ADOLF LOOS

The Viennese architect Adolf Loos (1870-1933) did not joint the Secession and criticised its members for the ornament and deliberate artiness of the furniture they designed. Loos greatly admired Roman architecture and

inherited from his stone-mason father a deep respect for 'raw' materials.

He travelled to the United States in 1893, the year after Louis Sullivan had published his *Ornament in Architecture*. Three years later Loos settled in Vienna, bringing with him a belief in the rejection of ornament (summed up in his essay 'Ornament and Crime' of 1908). Perhaps because of his outspoken stance, large scale commissions were slow to arrive, his most notable piece of design during this early period being the Kartner Bar of 1907. The apparent harshness of its geometric order is dissolved by the richness of shiny metals and lavish leather seating. Loos also designed bentwood chairs manufactured by Thonet for the Café Museum. He had been impressed by the work of the English Arts and Crafts Movement and several pieces he designed were of simple, panelled construction, marked by elegant proportions and a judicious disposition of simple reeding and metal fittings.

Loos designed a house for the Steiner family in Vienna in 1910 and this commission provided him with the opportunity to manifest his principles. The house is outstanding, not least because it is one of the first examples of domestic architecture to use reinforced concrete. Externally the building consists of smooth, flat walls of solid geometric blocks pierced by plate-glass windows (which are mainly horizontal) and a flat roof. Internally, the same geometric order prevails, but around an essentially traditional plan.

Loos went on to design many private villas before settling in Paris where he designed

Left: Armchair veneered in amboyna wood, designed by Kolomon Moser in 1904.

SPAIN
AND AMERICA

Above: Details of the polychromatic decoration which incorporates the Guell family monogram and coronet, by Catalan architect Antonio Gaudi.

Overleaf: The interior of Gaudi's mansion for Don Eusebio Guell. The interior shows the architect's interest in the ornate Gothic style, as well as Moorish-inspired design. They combine to produce a unique variation of the Art Nouveau style.

One of the strongest features of Art Nouveau was its very diversity. The remarkable set of characters, linked by common Art Nouveau traits, sets the short-lived movement apart from the homogeneity of previous styles, arid and easily transferred from master to pupil. The blossoming of Art Nouveau in Brussels, Glasgow, Paris, Munich, New York, Barcelona and so many other centres was a unanimous rejection of excessive uniformity.

GAUDI AND MODERNISMO

In both Belgium and France there were a number of architects working along similar lines, and Art Nouveau could lay claim to being a movement of sorts. In Spain Antonio Gaudi (1852-1926) worked in virtual isolation, and his only direct influences came from reading the works of Viollet-le-Duc, Ruskin and others. Yet Gaudi was arguably one of the most original and accomplished of all Art Nouveau architects.

Born in Tarragona, Gaudi moved to

Barcelona, the capital of Catalonia, around 1869, where he met his main patron, Eusebio Guell. Aside from the Neo-Gothic theories of Viollet-le-Duc, he was influenced by traditional Moorish and Moroccan styles, and by a mission to create a new Catalan architecture. His buildings were consequently more exotic than those of his contemporaries in northern Europe. In Gaudi's work one confronts one of the strangest variations of Art Nouveau, so firmly embedded in the peculiar local conditions that it is almost possible to see it as a purely local style. Indeed it even had its own name, *Modernismo*.

CATALAN TRADITION

Catalonia in particular had its own traditions. It was the wealthiest and most modern part of Spain, with its own industries and the thriving port of Barcelona, and was immensely proud of its trading history. These were vital to Catalan identity at a time when the central government in Madrid was attempting to integrate the region more completely into Spain, partly by discouraging the use of the native Catalan language. In this context of spirited Catalan patriotism, Gaudi began his architectural career as a Gothic Revivalist, but more specifically as a revivalist of the local Gothic style. This had its own element of fantasy, which Gaudi managed to emphasise through his study of the Moorish architecture of southern Spain and North Africa. To this, Gaudi added his knowledge of Viollet-le-Duc's work, with its light, almost tent like forms of iron-supported Gothic vaults. He was also inspired by John Ruskin's ideals of the unity

Right: Inside Gaudi's Church Santa Coloma de Cervello, for which he also designed the furniture.

Right: Mosaic decoration at the Parc Guell include broken tiles and old crockery.

Below: The ceramic mosaic-covered 'snake-bench' in the Parc Guell, designed by Antonio Gaudi.

of the arts and architecture making use of colour and carving more for its effects.

EARLY PATRONAGE

Gaudi was fortunate enough to have an outstanding patron for much of his work in the local shipping magnate Don Eusebio Guell, whose wealth allowed for very ambitious schemes. Gaudi's development was slow at first: his first work was the Casa Vicens, a city mansion built between 1878 and 1880, in which the most striking feature was the two massive parabolic arches of the portals filled by wrought-iron railings and gates modelled on a pattern of palm fronds. This was some of the most free-flowing ironwork decoration seen before Horta and Guimard.

Five years later he started the Palacio Guell, an extravagant town-house in which the decorative ironwork was accompanied by polychromatic glazed tiles and banded brickwork, and in which the first of Gaudi's twisted roof protuberances appeared.

The Chapel of Santa Coloma de Cervello, begun in 1898, incorporated a fantastic, rather nightmarish interior in which the jagged asymmetry was enhanced by leaning monolithic pillars, uneven vaults and a variety of raw textures and materials. This theme was continued in the Park Guell of 1900, while Gaudi took the principles of Art Nouveau to their architectural extreme in two apartment blocks begun in 1905, the Casa Battlo and the Casa Mila.

THE PARK GUELL

Perhaps inspired by the flowering of Art Nouveau in the rest of Europe, Gaudi's work of the 1890s began to develop into something unique, much more than just the sum of his early influences. Equally liberating must have been the scale on which he was invited to work by Guell.

A development of worker's houses did not get very far, but the centrepiece of a parallel scheme for a middle-class neighbourhood, the Park Guell, exists today as a municipal park. The Park Guell could be seen as a rare opportunity for the *Modernismo* artist to display his art against its source. Since this was a landscaping commission, Gaudi was able to employ the stylised, sinuous forms of Art Nouveau against the very natural shapes of the trees and flowers that had, in part, inspired them.

Serpentine paths did indeed weave throughout the park, but the centrepiece was a vast covered market roofed under a forest of mas-

Above: The 'snake bench' frames a public space which is supported by a series of columns.

Left: Detail of the wall of Gaudi's Parc Guell. The whole complex was designed at the behest of local ceramics manufacturer, Eusebio Guell. Gaudi's solutions are as potent expressions of the Art Nouveau style as seen anywhere in Europe.

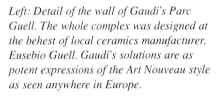

sive columns. On the plateau created above this area, Gaudi placed benches arranged in an almost continuous, undulating line from which the view of the city could be enjoyed. The backs of the benches were decorated with a mosaic of broken tiles arranged, either in patterns or haphazardly, to create a dazzlingly colourful display.

The same theme was continued on the roofs of the pavilions within the park, and, with further grottoes and concrete buttresses seemingly in the form of petrified treetrunks, the overall effect of the park is that of a strange mix of the subterranean and the maritime, perhaps appropriate for a city set between the sea and the mountains.

CASA BATTLO
The forms used within the fantastic realms of the Park Guell have justly been likened to enormously magnified versions of the Art Nouveau creations of Horta and Guimard, amplifying the air of strange, in this case, oversized, biological mutations. An interest in polychromatic effects gained through a combination of media, as in the Park Guell, was a frequent concern of Art Nouveau with characteristic ensembles of wood, metal and stained glass.

This interest was pursued by Gaudi in his Casa Battlo apartment block of 1905-7. The commission involved remodelling an existing block and the emphasis was inevitably on the facade. Gaudi had to contend with rectangular windows, already a part of the building and totally at odds with the shapes of Art Nouveau. In order to distract attention from them as well as exploit the shimmering light

Left: The amazing and unique staircase of the Casa Battlo with its bizarre vertebrae silhouette.

of a coastal city, coloured tiles were used again to create a flowing pattern throughout the facade, which was finished with a steep roof of titles coloured orange to blue-green. The brilliant colour effects enabled Gaudi to move away from the more symmetrically-composed facades of the neighbouring houses. By means of a rather exotic turret and the fabric-like folds of the roof, the Casa Battlo also managed to rise above its companions in the street.

The base of the building was reworked by using a stone cladding whose flowing lines and softly modelled protuberances seemed closer to underwater life than to architecture. Some of the remaining windows on the upper storeys received bizarrely shaped iron balconies, somewhat resembling fish skeletons.

THE CASA MILA

While the Casa Battlo was concerned with a rather two-dimensional presentation, the Casa Mila apartments, completely designed by Gaudi, received a much more plastic, virtually sculptural treatment. Rapidly named 'La Pedera' (the quarry) by the locals, Casa Mila seems to allude to many natural sources. Like a cliff face or a rock outcrop eroded by the wind into a collection of grottoes or tunnels, it seems to have been converted to human habitation only at some late stage in its history.

Even in plan the Casa Mila appears like some cellular organism rather than the work of an architect, and the internal structure, was indeed, only resolved at a late stage by the use of partitions.

As Gaudi's career developed, it is possible that he increasingly abandoned architectural drawings and worked at first-hand with his

Right: The Casa Mila, with its wrought iron balconies that recall tangled seaweed.

Above: Dressing table designed for the Palacio Guell, Barcelona by Gaudi, 1890.

Right: The honeycomb surface of the (still unfinished) Cathedral of the Sagrada Familia in Barcelona.

craftsmen, like a latter-day William Morris. Certainly he became much less reliant on iron and glass than Horta or Guimard, as is evident in the Casa Mila. Instead, the effect of erosion is produced by careful carving of each block of the stone facade. In total contrast to this softness is the ironwork of the balconies which is moulded into intricately twisted plant forms, like seaweed hanging from the cliff face before the next wave breaks upon it.

SAGRADA FAMILIA

Gaudi's great Barcelona church, the still-to-be finished Sagrada Familia, occupied him for his entire career, and like the Casa Mila, it is an example of extreme Art Nouveau fantasy enlarged into monumental three dimensions. It is also a typical combination of the reactionary and revolutionary, stemming from Gaudi's extremely devout Roman Catholicism, here given a form of unique novelty: Gothic seen through Art Nouveau eyes of the late 19th century.

GAUDI'S FURNITURE

For many of his buildings Gaudi designed equally extraordinary, idiosyncratic furniture. Among surviving examples are pieces designed for the Chapel of Santa Coloma de Cervello, the Casa Calvert, built from 1898-1904 and for the Casa Battlo.

The style of the furniture is consistent: organic 'shell-and-bone' forms are the most obvious. One extraordinary piece, (the authenticity of which is doubtful, however), is an ornate prayer stool believed to have been part of the furnishings for the Casa Battlo. The rich 'acajou et bois de loup' base of the stool, with upholstered platforms for the knees and elbows, was surmounted by an edifice of stained glass embellished by five large gilt-

bronze roses. Although very Spanish in feel, the piece bears little resemblance to known examples of Gaudi's furniture.

ART NOUVEAU IN AMERICA

In the main, the decorative arts in America in the 19th century took their lead from Europe, whether from Greek classicism or Louis-Quinze, and these revivalist tendencies were also adopted in architecture. But the United States led the world in technical virtuosity and in the far-sightedness of many of its designers and patrons.

Contemporary movements in Europe tended to reach America somewhat anachronistically and haphazardly. The Gothic Revival of Ruskin reached America merely as a style to be adopted by a few designers, and lacked both the emotional and nationalistic fervour of the English movement. The opening up of Japan, however, and the resultant Aesthetic Movement, did capture America's artistic imagination.

ARTS AND CRAFTS IN AMERICA

By 1890 the most important foreign importation of style was the Arts and Crafts Movement of Morris and Ruskin. Many Americans had visited England and met Morris personally before returning home, fired with his ideals, dedicated to handicrafts and the rejection of the machine in art. Publications such as *International Studio*, *House Beautiful*, *The Ladies Home Journal* and *The Craftsman* spread the word to an even wider audience.

The Arts and Crafts Movement was important in America not only for the fine workmanship it encouraged from individuals, but also for the growing awareness it developed among Americans that they should also find a truly national art. But

Above: A wooden armchair designed by Gaudi for the Casa Calvert, Barcelona, in 1902.

THE ROYCROFT SHOP IN EAST AVRORA

Left: Oak chair by the American designer Charles Rohlfs, 1898.

Above: Print of the Roycroft Shops of Hubbard's crafts community in East Aurora, near Buffalo, New York.

the concepts of national art did, in fact, differ across the country. On the East Coast, Morris-inspired communities were founded and furniture and other decorative items made which have a direct resemblance to the British movement. On the West Coast, however, the climate and the landscape led to different interpretations. Morris's romantic return to the medieval European past was supplanted in California by the recognition of its own past in Spanish-Mexican and Native American culture.

CRAFTSMEN COMMUNITIES AND WORKSHOPS

One of the first to assimilate European trends in design was Charles Rohlfs who opened a small workshop in Buffalo in 1890 and his work reflects both the 'Mission Style' of California and Art Nouveau in elaborate carving and detailing, mainly in oak. Rohlfs often lectured at the Roycroft community at East Aurora, which had been started by Elbert Hubbard in 1895.

Roycroft was run along business lines, beginning with a press and book bindery, and gradually incorporating other crafts. Around 1901, the furniture shop was started. Solidly and honestly made, generally in oak or mahogany, early works were heavier versions of chairs by Morris & Co., while later pieces resembled the Craftsman style of Gustav Stickley (1857-1942).

STICKLEY AND *THE CRAFTSMAN*

Following his debt to Ruskin and absorbing the principles of his architecture, in 1901 Stickley founded *The Craftsman* magazine in which he upheld the social aims of the British Arts and Crafts designers and called for a truly democratic national art. Stickley believed in a quasi-psychological view that more simple surroundings would lead to spiritual regeneration, especially in industrial cities, and his solid, severe furniture seems to reflect his social aims.

THE CHICAGO SCHOOL

A genuine American style was to be forged through the work of Louis Sullivan (1856-1924) and Frank Lloyd Wright (1867-1959) in Chicago. Sullivan had introduced Art Nouveau forms in a system of architectural ornament, holding that the outward form of a building should be expressive of its function. Sullivan's best work was for office buildings, but his ideas were taken and expanded by Wright into residential buildings.

Wright believed in integral design for his houses, and his furniture was designed to solve specific problems within a particular interior, as in the Hanna House where the polygonal furniture reflects the hexagonal design of the house. Each house also had a particular ornamental theme and any added decoration was to echo that chosen motif; decoration for Wright generally relied on positioning geometric shapes.

Perhaps the most important centre of Arts and Crafts activity was Chicago. In an area

Right: A cover of The Craftsman *magazine.*

THE CRAFTSMAN

VOL. V   JANUARY·1904   NO. 4

COPY 25 CENTS   PUBLISHED MONTHLY BY THE UNITED CRAFTS SYRACUSE·N·Y·-U·S·A·   YEAR 3 DOLLARS

Above: A Craftsman living room as illustrated in the magazine, The Craftsman *which was founded by Gustav Stickley in 1901.*

most affected by frontier concepts, a style had to be evolved which no longer took its lead from the commercial and organisational centres of the East Coast, rooted as they were in European traditions. The Midwest relied on modern machines and means of communications for its survival, and could, even in the 1890s, ill afford to espouse the microcosmic ideals of the Arts and Crafts Movement. The

movement did, however, supply the impetus for a freedom of style.

LOUIS SULLIVAN

Louis Sullivan was the leader of the innovative group of architects based in the booming city of Chicago and his importance as a pioneer of 20th century architecture extends well beyond the isolated decade or so of Art

Above: Stickley is best known for his strong sturdy designs intended to evoke the 'simple life' of the early pioneers. This fall front, wooden desk is typical is typical of his work.

Left: A redwood side chair by Frank Lloyd Wright for the Paul R. Hanna House (The Honeycomb House) in Palo Alto, California, 1937.

Nouveau. Sullivan led the movement towards the exploitation of the new steel-framed structures, which, with the development of the elevator, enabled him to produce some of the most successful early skyscrapers.

STRUCTURAL SKELETON

Sullivan's architecture is more concerned with expressing the structural skeleton of a building, by allowing a very simple grid-form to appear as the basic design, and by hollowing out the ground floor until it rests on just a few reinforced columns. These innovations of Sullivan's were eventually to become commonplace in modern architecture throughout the world.

ORNAMENTATION

Yet Sullivan remained very much a man of his time in his attitude towards the embellishment of his buildings. His theories on the subject were highly developed, and he saw the contrast between the rectilinear and the curvilinear as parallel to the division between intellect and emotion. Throughout his architectural career he tried to maintain a balance between the two.

The actual form of his ornament was often reminiscent of oriental abstractions from nature, but just as frequently he used more overt natural forms of intertwining leaves and branches which became very much a Chicago version of Art Nouveau: home-grown, but with very strong formal links with the style as it had developed in Europe.

The bar interior of the great Auditorium Building, a complex of opera house, hotel and offices, shows an opulence of detail and the involvement of the architect in every small feature which is characteristic of Art Nouveau. Nor was Sullivan averse to turning his bare exposed vertical beams, part of his grid facade, into rather exotic tree forms by using a flourish of foliage at the top, as in the facade of the Gage Building of South Michigan Avenue in Chicago.

More frequently, Sullivan preferred to contain very lush and flowing natural ornament within quite rigid limits, as in the Wainwright Building in St. Louis, where it serves to articulate the horizontal beams set against the plain verticals, and to embellish a very ornate cornice which caps the whole composition.

The natural forms of Sullivan's decoration not only recalled those of French Art Nouveau, but also had symbolic importance for him. The energy of organic growth was what Sullivan was attempting to evoke, and in particular, its application to the rapidly developing cities of America. Just as Art Nouveau was self-consciously the 'modern style', so Sullivan was attempting to create a powerful, growing architecture.

GOTHIC FANTASY

His Guaranty Building in Buffalo, New York, extends this Art Nouveau concern for growth beyond the decoration itself, into the structure as a whole. Linked by arches at their peak, the great verticals of the building seem to be enormous stems pushing up to the cornice which curls over in a gentle curve reminiscent of growing form. In this case, the

Far left: In structure, Louis Sullivan's Carson, Pirie Scott department store in Chicago, Illinois, anticipates much of 20th century architecture.

Left: Louis Sullivan's Auditorium Building whose austere facade contrasts with the lavishness of some of the interior decoration.

ornament makes the analogies more explicit.

Sullivan's last work, the then Carson, Pirie & Scott department store in Chicago, seems for the main area of the facade to be too plain for any reference to Art Nouveau to be made, yet in the first two storeys, and particularly around the corner entrance, there is relief work of Gaudi-like extravagance, which, even in this unlikely context, recalls Sagrada Familia. This seems largely based on an elaborate Gothic fantasy, yet its tense spider web lines and twisting foliage can ultimately only be seen as a personal Art Nouveau composition.

Left: The decorative metalwork over the Carson, Pirie Scott store recalls the florid exuberance of Art Nouveau.